Christmas miniatures

finger food and tiny treats

THE AUSTRALIAN
Women's Weekly

CONTENTS

AUSTRALIAN CUP AND
SPOON MEASUREMENTS
ARE METRIC.
A CONVERSION CHART
APPEARS ON PAGE 77.

I love this collection of little Christmas bites -
they are fun, colourful and elegant all at once.
You'll see how easy it is to turn a small cake
or biscuit into a pretty jewelled treat, and how
to make our traditional Christmas favourites
look and taste extra-special.

Pamela Clark

Food Director

ZUCCHINI AND CORN FRITTERS WITH CREME FRAICHE

prep + cook time **40 minutes (+ standing)** makes **50**

½ cup (75g) plain (all-purpose) flour
½ cup (75g) self-raising flour
2 eggs
½ cup (140g) yogurt
½ teaspoon caster (superfine) sugar
420g (13½ ounces) canned corn
   kernels, drained
2 small zucchini (180g), grated coarsely
2 cloves garlic, crushed
1 small red onion (100g), chopped finely
2 tablespoons finely chopped fresh basil
1 tablespoon finely chopped fresh tarragon
¼ cup (20g) finely grated parmesan cheese
2 tablespoons olive oil
¾ cup (180g) crème fraîche
⅓ cup (50g) pine nuts, roasted
⅓ cup fresh baby basil leaves

1 Combine flours in large bowl; whisk in eggs, yogurt and sugar. Stir in corn, zucchini, garlic, onion, chopped herbs and cheese; stand 15 minutes.
2 Heat oil in large frying pan; cook heaped teaspoons of mixture, in batches, until browned both sides. Cool on wire racks.
3 Serve fritters topped with crème fraîche, pine nuts and basil leaves.

tips Fresh corn can be used instead of canned corn; you will need 2 cobs. Sour cream or yogurt can be used instead of the crème fraîche. Fritters can be made the day before; top them with crème fraîche etc, an hour or so before serving.

COCKTAIL
FOOD

sticky-glazed pork with pineapple

GREEN ONION BLINIS WITH CHILLI CRAB SALAD

prep + cook time **40 minutes (+ cooling)** makes **24**

⅔ cup (100g) wholemeal plain
    (all-purpose) flour
⅓ cup (50g) white self-raising flour
½ teaspoon cayenne pepper
2 eggs
¾ cup (180ml) buttermilk
2 green onions (scallions), sliced finely
40g (1½ ounces) butter, melted
chilli crab salad
150g (4½ ounces) cooked crab meat
1 tablespoon each finely chopped fresh mint
    and vietnamese mint
1 teaspoon finely grated lime rind
2 tablespoons lime juice
2 teaspoons fish sauce
½ lebanese cucumber (65g), seeded,
    chopped finely
1 fresh small red thai (serrano) chilli,
    sliced thinly

1 Sift flours and pepper into medium bowl; whisk in eggs and buttermilk until smooth. Stir in onion and butter.
2 Heat oiled large frying pan; cook level tablespoons of blini mixture, in batches, until golden both sides. Cool on wire racks.
3 Meanwhile, make chilli crab salad.
4 Serve blinis topped with salad.
chilli crab salad Combine ingredients in medium bowl; season to taste.

tip You could serve the crab mixture on mini toasts, lavosh crispbreads or sliced french bread stick.

STICKY-GLAZED PORK WITH PINEAPPLE

prep + cook time **25 minutes (+ refrigeration)** makes **32**

2 pork fillets (600g)
2 tablespoons char siu sauce
1 tablespoon light soy sauce
½ small pineapple (450g), sliced thinly
½ cup (25g) snow pea sprouts, trimmed

1 Combine pork and sauces in large bowl. Cover; refrigerate 1 hour.
2 Cook pineapple on heated oiled grill plate (or grill or barbecue) until browned lightly. Remove from grill, cover to keep warm. Halve slices.
3 Cook pork over low heat on grill plate, covered, about 10 minutes or until cooked. Cover; stand 5 minutes then slice thinly.
4 Top pineapple with 2 slices of pork then sprouts.

tip We served these bites on small squares of banana leaf, making them easier to handle. The pineapple was cut in half lengthways, then sliced thinly.

green onion blinis with chilli crab salad

vodka-cured gravlax

VODKA-CURED GRAVLAX

prep time 10 minutes (+ refrigeration) makes 24

1 tablespoon sea salt
1 teaspoon finely ground black pepper
1 tablespoon white (granulated) sugar
1 tablespoon vodka
300g (9½-ounce) salmon fillet, skin on
24 mini toasts
sour cream sauce
⅓ cup (80g) sour cream
2 teaspoons rinsed, drained baby capers
2 teaspoons lemon juice
2 teaspoons finely chopped drained
    cornichons
½ small red onion (50g), chopped finely

1 Combine salt, pepper, sugar and vodka in small bowl.
2 Remove any bones from fish; place fish, skin-side down, on piece of plastic wrap. Spread vodka mixture over top of fish; wrap securely in plastic. Refrigerate overnight, turning parcel several times.
3 Make sour cream sauce.
4 Slice fish thinly; spread sauce on toasts, top with fish.
sour cream sauce Combine ingredients in small bowl; season to taste.

SMOKED CHICKEN CROSTINI

prep + cook time 30 minutes makes 24

1½ cups (180g) shredded smoked chicken
2 shallots (50g), chopped finely
¼ cup (30g) finely chopped celery
¼ cup (25g) walnuts, roasted,
    chopped coarsely
1 tablespoon finely chopped fresh tarragon
¼ cup (75g) mayonnaise
1 teaspoon wholegrain mustard
1 tablespoon preserved lemon rind,
    chopped finely
1 small french bread stick (150g),
    cut into 24 slices
1 large clove garlic, halved
2 tablespoons olive oil
1 small pear (180g), cut into matchsticks

smoked chicken crostini

1 Combine chicken, shallot, celery, nuts, tarragon, mayonnaise, mustard and preserved lemon in medium bowl; season to taste.
2 Toast bread slices, in batches, on heated grill plate (or grill or barbecue). Rub one side with garlic, brush with oil.
3 Serve crostini topped with chicken mixture and pear.

tips Chicken mixture can be prepared a day ahead; keep covered in the refrigerator. Preserved lemons can be bought from delis and some supermarkets. Remove a piece of lemon from the jar, discard the lemon flesh. Rinse the rind under water, dry, then chop finely.

camembert with pear compote on pumpernickel

SCALLOPS WITH SAFFRON CREAM

prep + cook time **15 minutes (+ standing)** makes **12**

12 scallops in half shell (480g)
1 teaspoon olive oil
1 small brown onion (80g), chopped finely
2 teaspoons finely grated lemon rind
pinch saffron threads
⅔ cup (160ml) pouring cream
1 tablespoon lemon juice
2 teaspoons salmon roe

1 Remove scallops from shells; wash and dry shells. Place shells, in single layer, on serving platter.
2 Rinse scallops under cold water; discard scallop roe. Gently pat scallops dry with absorbent paper.
3 Heat oil in small saucepan; cook onion, stirring, until softened. Add rind, saffron and cream; bring to the boil. Reduce heat; simmer, uncovered, about 5 minutes or until mixture has reduced to about ½ cup. Remove from heat; stand 30 minutes. Stir in juice, season to taste; stand 10 minutes. Strain cream mixture into small bowl then back into same cleaned pan; stir over low heat until heated through.
4 Meanwhile, cook scallops, in batches, on heated oiled grill plate (or grill or barbecue) until browned lightly and cooked as desired.
5 Return scallops to shells; top with cream sauce and salmon roe.

CAMEMBERT WITH PEAR COMPOTE ON PUMPERNICKEL

prep + cook time **20 minutes (+ cooling)** makes **24**

2 tablespoons dried cranberries, chopped finely
1 cinnamon stick
½ cup (75g) dried pears, chopped finely
1 tablespoon caster (superfine) sugar
¼ cup (60ml) water
200g (6½-ounce) whole camembert cheese
24 cocktail pumpernickel rounds (250g)
1 tablespoon roasted pistachios, chopped finely

1 Combine cranberries, cinnamon, pear, sugar and the water in small saucepan; bring to the boil. Reduce heat; simmer, uncovered, 10 minutes. Cool; discard cinnamon.
2 Cut cheese into 24 wedges.
3 Place pumpernickel rounds on serving platter; top each round with a wedge of cheese, ½ teaspoon of the compote then a sprinkle of nuts.

scallops with saffron cream

CHICKEN AND PORT PATE ON POLENTA CRISPS

prep + cook time 50 minutes (+ refrigeration) makes 48

50g (1½ ounces) butter, softened
300g (9½ ounces) chicken livers, trimmed
2 shallots (50g), chopped finely
1 clove garlic, crushed
2 tablespoons port
48 (approximately 100g) drained seeded
   sour cherries
48 fresh chervil sprigs
polenta crisps
1 cup (250ml) water
2 cups (500ml) chicken stock
¾ cup (125g) polenta
30g (1 ounce) butter
vegetable oil, for deep-frying

1 Make polenta crisps.

2 Meanwhile, heat half the butter in medium frying pan; cook livers, in batches, until just browned. Remove from pan.

3 Cook shallot and garlic in same pan, stirring, until shallot softens. Add port; cook, uncovered, until almost all of the liquid has evaporated.

4 Blend or process livers with shallot mixture until smooth. Push mixture through sieve; discard solids.

5 Blend or process pâté mixture with remaining butter until smooth. Transfer to small bowl, cover; refrigerate pâté 2 hours.

6 Serve pâté on polenta crisps; top each with a cherry and a sprig of chervil.

polenta crisps Oil 8cm x 25cm (3¼-inch x 10-inch) bar cake pan. Combine the water and stock in medium saucepan, bring to the boil; gradually add polenta, stirring constantly. Reduce heat; simmer, stirring, about 10 minutes or until polenta thickens. Stir in butter, season to taste, then spread polenta into prepared pan; cool 10 minutes. Cover; refrigerate about 2 hours or until firm. Trim edges; cut in half lengthways, then slice into 1cm (½-inch) pieces. Heat oil in wok; deep-fry polenta, in batches, until browned. Drain on absorbent paper.

SPICED EGGPLANT AND HALOUMI TARTS

prep + cook time **50 minutes** makes **30**

1 medium eggplant (300g), peeled,
  chopped coarsely
1 teaspoon each ground cumin and
  ground coriander
2 tablespoons olive oil
¼ cup (55g) firmly packed light brown sugar
¼ cup (60ml) water
¼ cup (60ml) lime juice
2 tablespoons finely chopped fresh
  flat-leaf parsley
100g (3 ounces) haloumi cheese,
  sliced thickly
2 tablespoons lemon juice
1 teaspoon finely cracked black pepper
30 baked mini shortcrust or puff pastry
  tart shells
2 tablespoons finely shredded lime rind

1 Preheat oven to 200°C/400°F.
2 Toss eggplant, cumin, coriander and oil in small baking dish; season. Cover dish; roast 20 minutes. Uncover; roast about 10 minutes or until eggplant is tender.
3 Combine sugar and the water in small saucepan; stir over heat until sugar dissolves.
4 Blend or process eggplant mixture, sugar syrup and lime juice until eggplant is coarsely chopped. Stir in parsley; cover to keep warm.
5 Sprinkle cheese with lemon juice and pepper; cook on heated barbecue (or grill or grill plate) until browned both sides. Chop cheese into 30 pieces.
6 Meanwhile, fill tart shells with warm eggplant mixture; top with cheese and lime rind.

tips Mini shortcrust and puff pastry tart shells are available from most major supermarkets and delis. For an earthier flavour, barbecue the whole eggplant. First prick the skin all over with a fork, then cook the eggplant for about 30 minutes – depending on its size and the heat of the barbecue – or until the eggplant collapses. Cool the eggplant, peel away the skin, then proceed with the recipe.

roast beef with caramelised onion on rye

ROAST BEEF WITH CARAMELISED ONION ON RYE

prep + cook time **50 minutes** makes **40**

500g (1-pound) beef fillet
1 tablespoon olive oil
2 large red onions (600g), sliced thinly
1 tablespoon light brown sugar
1 tablespoon red wine vinegar
1 loaf rye bread (660g)
¼ cup (60ml) olive oil, extra
2 tablespoons mild english mustard
⅓ cup finely chopped fresh flat-leaf parsley

1 Preheat oven to 180°C/350°F.
2 Cook beef in heated, oiled medium frying pan until browned all over; place in small baking dish. Roast, uncovered, in oven, about 20 minutes or until cooked. Wrap beef in foil.
3 Heat oil in same pan; cook onion, stirring, until soft. Add sugar and vinegar; cook, stirring, until onion is caramelised.
4 Preheat grill (broiler). If not already sliced, cut bread into 1.5cm (¾-inch) slices; cut each slice into quarters. Brush bread, both sides, with extra oil; toast both sides under grill.
5 Slice beef thinly. Spread mustard on bread; top with beef and onion, sprinkle with parsley.

asian oysters

ASIAN OYSTERS

prep time **30 minutes (+ refrigeration)** makes **24**

24 oysters, on the half shell
¼ cup (60ml) lime juice
1 tablespoon fish sauce
2 teaspoons white (granulated) sugar
2 tablespoons coconut cream
1 baby brown onion (25g), sliced thinly
1 fresh long red chilli, sliced thinly
2 tablespoons each finely chopped fresh
    coriander (cilantro) and mint

1 Remove oysters from shells; discard shells.
2 Combine oysters in medium bowl with juice, sauce and sugar; cover, refrigerate 1 hour. Stir in coconut cream.
3 Combine onion, chilli and herbs in small bowl.
4 Place Chinese spoons on serving platter. Place 1 undrained oyster on each spoon; top with herb mixture.

MINI PRAWN COCKTAIL

prep time **20 minutes**

Flavour mayonnaise with dashes of tomato sauce, worcestershire sauce, Tabasco and horseradish cream; season to taste. Fill baby lettuce leaves with shelled cooked prawns; top with mayonnaise mixture, chopped chives and finely grated lemon rind.

SMOKED SALMON CANAPES

prep time **15 minutes**

Flavour sour cream with finely chopped fresh dill, finely grated lemon rind, finely chopped red onion and chopped, drained and rinsed baby capers; season to taste. Spread sour cream mixture onto mini toasts. Top with smoked salmon and dill sprigs.

NO-FUSS FINGER FOOD

QUAIL EGGS WITH DUKKAH

prep + cook time **15 minutes**

Place quail eggs in a single layer in wide
saucepan. Barely cover eggs with water; cover,
bring to the boil. Boil for 1½ minutes; drain
eggs, rinse with cold water. Crack shell of each
egg; place eggs in bowl of cold water. Shell
eggs under cold water. Sprinkle eggs with
dukkah; serve on a bed of sea salt flakes
sprinkled with chervil sprigs.

CHICKEN WONTON CRISPS

prep + cook time **30 minutes**

Cut each wonton wrapper into four squares;
deep-fry until crisp. Combine shredded smoked
chicken with finely chopped apple and green
onions, mayonnaise and mustard; season to
taste. Spoon onto cooled wonton crisps.

FRUIT MINCE PIES
WITH SPICED HAZELNUT PASTRY

prep + cook time 1 hour (+ refrigeration & cooling)
makes 18

1½ cups (225g) plain (all-purpose) flour
¾ cup (75g) ground hazelnuts
½ cup (80g) icing (confectioners') sugar
2 teaspoons mixed spice
185g (6 ounces) cold butter,
   chopped coarsely
1 egg yolk
2 teaspoons iced water, approximately
1½ cups (375g) fruit mince
2 teaspoons finely grated orange rind
1 egg, beaten lightly

1 Process flour, ground hazelnuts, sugar, spice and butter until crumbly. With motor operating, add egg yolk and enough of the water to make ingredients come together. Knead dough on floured surface until smooth. Wrap pastry in plastic; refrigerate 30 minutes.
2 Preheat oven to 220°C/425°F. Grease 18 holes of two 12-hole (2-tablespoon/40ml) deep flat-based patty pans.
3 Roll out half the pastry between sheets of baking paper until 5mm (¼ inch) thick. Cut out nine 7.5cm (3-inch) fluted rounds; press rounds into pan holes. Repeat with remaining pastry.
4 Combine fruit mince and rind in medium bowl; spoon mince mixture into cases, brush edges of pastry with egg. Roll scraps of pastry on floured surface, until 5mm (¼ inch) thick. Cut out 18 x 5cm (2-inch) fluted rounds. Cut 2cm (¾-inch) fluted rounds from centre of the rounds. Top pies with rounds.
5 Bake pies about 25 minutes. Stand pies in pan 10 minutes; transfer to wire rack to cool. Dust with a little extra sifted icing sugar.

LITTLE PIES & TARTS

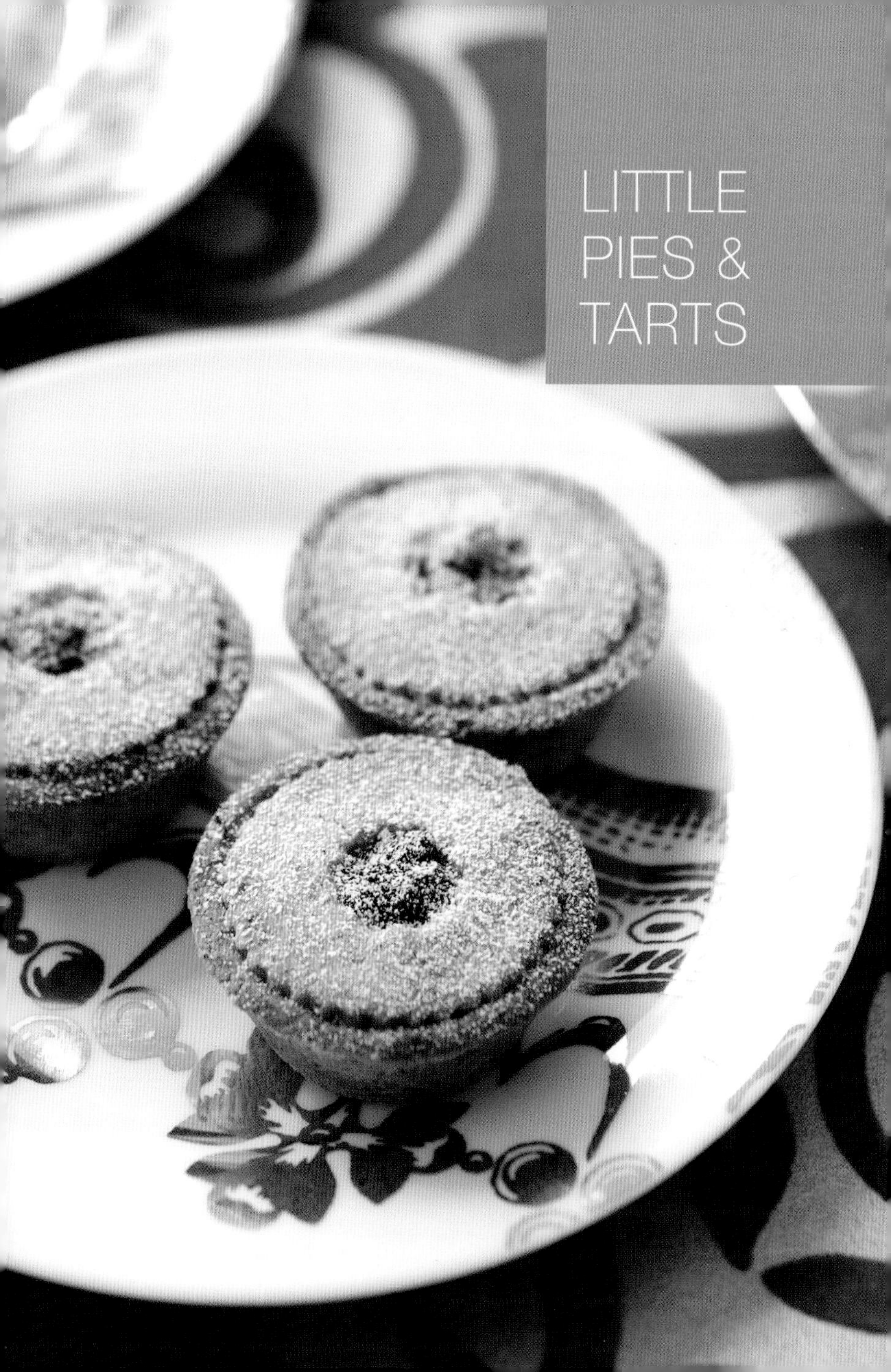

ECCLES MINCE PIES

prep + cook time **1 hour (+ refrigeration)** makes **63**

7 sheets puff pastry
1 egg white, beaten lightly
1½ tablespoons white (granulated) sugar
fruit mince
1 cup (150g) raisins
1 cup (160g) dried currants
1 cup (160g) sultanas
1 slice (35g) dried pineapple
2 tablespoons glacé cherries
¼ cup (40g) blanched almonds
1 large apple (200g), grated coarsely
½ cup (110g) lightly packed light brown sugar
50g (1½ ounces) butter, melted
1 tablespoon finely grated orange rind
¼ cup (60ml) orange juice
¼ cup (60ml) brandy
½ teaspoon mixed spice

1 Make fruit mince.
2 Preheat oven to 200°C/400°F. Line three oven trays with baking paper.
3 Cut each pastry sheet into nine squares. Top each with heaped teaspoons of fruit mince; brush pastry edges with egg white. Gather sides of pastry together to encase filling; turn pies upside down onto trays. Gently flatten pies; cut two slits in top of pies. Brush pies with egg white; sprinkle with sugar.
4 Bake pies about 15 minutes or until golden brown.

fruit mince Process dried fruit and nuts until coarsely chopped. Transfer mixture to large bowl; stir in remaining ingredients. Refrigerate, covered, at least 2 days, stirring daily.

tips Fruit mince will keep for at least 3 months in an airtight container in the refrigerator. The flavours will intensify the longer it is left before using. This recipe makes about 3½ cups. You can also use ready-made fruit mince if you're running out of time. You can fill and shape the pies, and freeze in an airtight container for up to 2 months. Brush frozen pies with egg white, sprinkle with sugar and bake about 20 minutes.

FIG MINCE PIES

prep + cook time **1 hour 40 minutes**
(+ standing & refrigeration) makes **24**

150g (4½ ounces) dried figs, chopped finely
½ cup (65g) dried cranberries
½ cup (75g) raisins, chopped coarsely
¼ cup (40g) mixed peel
¼ cup (55g) finely chopped glacé ginger
¼ cup (60g) finely chopped glacé peach
1 medium apple (150g), grated coarsely
½ cup (110g) firmly packed light brown sugar
2 tablespoons fig jam
1 teaspoon finely grated orange rind
2 tablespoons orange juice
1 cinnamon stick, halved
1 teaspoon mixed spice
⅓ cup (80ml) brandy
1½ sheets shortcrust pastry
1 egg white, beaten lightly
pastry
2 cups (300g) plain (all-purpose) flour
⅓ cup (75g) caster (superfine) sugar
150g (4½ ounces) cold butter,
    chopped coarsely
1 egg

1 Combine fruit, sugar, jam, rind, juice, spices and brandy in medium bowl. Cover; stand for one week or up to one month. Stir mixture every two or three days.
2 Make pastry.
3 Grease two 12-hole (2-tablespoon/40ml) deep flat-based patty pans. Roll out half the pastry between sheets of baking paper until 3mm (⅛ inch) thick. Cut out twelve 7cm (2¾-inch) rounds; press rounds into holes of one pan. Prick bases of cases well with a fork. Repeat with remaining pastry. Refrigerate 30 minutes.
4 Preheat oven to 200°C/400°F.
5 Cut the whole pastry sheet into 16 squares; cut each square into six strips. Cut the half pastry sheet into eight squares; cut each square into six strips.
6 Use six pastry strips to weave a lattice pattern. Cut a 6.5cm (2½-inch) round from latticed pastry. Repeat with remaining pastry strips.
7 Discard cinnamon stick from mince. Spoon mince into pastry cases; top with lattice pastry rounds. Press edges to seal; brush pastry with egg white. Bake about 20 minutes. Dust with a little sifted icing (confectioners') sugar, if you like, before serving.
pastry Process flour, sugar and butter until crumbly. Add egg; process until combined. Knead dough on floured surface until smooth. Wrap pastry in plastic; refrigerate 30 minutes.

tips **Mince pies will keep well in an airtight container for up to two weeks. Make double the quantity of fruit mince to bottle for gifts.**

APPLE CHERRY PIES

prep + cook time **1 hour (+ refrigeration & cooling)**
makes **18**

3 medium apples (450g), peeled,
    chopped finely
¼ cup (55g) caster (superfine) sugar
1 star anise
2 tablespoons water
300g (9½ ounces) frozen seeded cherries,
    quartered
1 tablespoon cornflour (cornstarch)
1 egg white, beaten lightly
2 teaspoons caster (superfine) sugar, extra
pastry
1⅔ cups (250g) plain (all-purpose) flour
⅓ cup (75g) caster (superfine) sugar
150g (4½ ounces) cold butter,
    chopped coarsely
1 egg yolk

1 Make pastry.
2 Combine apple, sugar, star anise and half
the water in medium saucepan; bring to the
boil. Reduce heat; simmer, covered, about
5 minutes or until apple is tender. Add cherries;
simmer 2 minutes. Stir in blended cornflour and
the remaining water; stir over heat until mixture
boils and thickens. Remove from heat; cool
10 minutes. Discard star anise.
3 Preheat oven to 200°C/400°F. Grease
18 holes of two 12-hole (2-tablespoon/40ml)
deep flat-based patty pans.
4 Roll two-thirds of the pastry between sheets
of baking paper until 3mm (⅛ inch) thick; cut
out 18 x 6.5cm (2¾-inch) rounds from pastry.
Press rounds into pan holes. Refrigerate
20 minutes.
5 Roll remaining pastry between sheets of
baking paper to make a 20cm (8-inch) square;
cut into 5mm (¼-inch) wide strips. Spoon fruit
mixture into cases, brush edges of pastry with
egg white. Lattice pastry strips over fruit filling;
trim any excess pastry. Brush lattice with egg
white; sprinkle with extra sugar. Bake about
20 minutes.
6 Stand pies in pan 10 minutes; transfer to
wire rack to cool.
pastry Process flour, sugar and butter until
crumbly. Add egg yolk; process until combined.
Knead dough on floured surface until smooth.
Wrap pastry in plastic; refrigerate 30 minutes.

custard fruit tarts

CUSTARD FRUIT TARTS

prep + cook time **1 hour (+ refrigeration & cooling)**
makes **24**

1¾ cups (260g) plain (all-purpose) flour
¼ cup (40g) icing (confectioners') sugar
185g (6 ounces) cold butter,
   chopped coarsely
1 egg yolk
2 teaspoons iced water, approximately
1 medium kiwifruit (85g)
60g (2 ounces) fresh raspberries, halved
60g (2 ounces) fresh blueberries
custard cream
1 cup (250ml) milk
1 teaspoon vanilla extract
3 egg yolks
⅓ cup (75g) caster (superfine) sugar
2 tablespoons cornflour (cornstarch)
⅓ cup (80ml) thickened (heavy) cream,
   whipped

1 Process flour, sugar and butter until crumbly. With motor operating, add egg yolk and enough of the water to make ingredients come together. Knead dough on floured surface until smooth. Wrap pastry in plastic; refrigerate 30 minutes.
2 Grease two 12-hole (1-tablespoon/20ml) mini muffin pans. Roll out half the pastry between sheets of baking paper until 3mm (⅛ inch) thick. Cut out twelve 6cm (2½-inch) rounds; press rounds into holes of one pan. Prick bases of cases well with a fork. Repeat with remaining pastry. Refrigerate 30 minutes.
3 Preheat oven to 200°C/400°F.
4 Bake cases about 10 minutes. Stand cases in pan 5 minutes; transfer to wire rack to cool.
5 Meanwhile, make custard cream.
6 Cut kiwifruit crossways into eight slices; cut 3cm (1¼-inch) rounds from slices. Spoon custard cream into cases; top with fruit.
custard cream Bring milk and extract to the boil in small saucepan. Beat egg yolks, sugar and cornflour in small bowl with electric mixer until thick. With motor operating, gradually beat in hot milk mixture. Return custard to same pan; stir over heat until mixture boils and thickens. Cover surface of custard with plastic wrap; refrigerate 1 hour. Fold cream into custard.

tips **Pastry cases and custard cream can be made and stored separately, 2 days ahead; fold cream into custard just before using. Assemble and serve tarts as close to serving time as possible – about an hour is good.**

SPICY CHRISTMAS CUPCAKES

prep + cook time 1 hour (+ standing) makes 12

90g (3 ounces) butter, softened
1 egg
¼ cup (60ml) buttermilk
2 tablespoons golden syrup or treacle
½ cup (110g) firmly packed light brown sugar
½ cup (75g) plain (all-purpose) flour
½ cup (75g) self-raising flour
¼ teaspoon bicarbonate of soda (baking soda)
1 teaspoon ground ginger
½ teaspoon ground cinnamon
¼ teaspoon ground nutmeg
Christmas decorations
½ cup (80g) icing (confectioners') sugar
125g (4 ounces) ready-made white icing
various shaped Christmas cutters
5cm (2-inch) lengths of covered
    24 gauge wire
fruit mince filling
½ cup (125g) fruit mince
1 tablespoon icing (confectioners') sugar

1 Make Christmas decorations.
2 Preheat oven to 180°C/350°F. Line 12-hole
(⅓-cup/80ml) muffin pan with paper cases.
3 Beat butter, egg, buttermilk, syrup, sugar and
sifted dry ingredients in small bowl with electric
mixer on low speed until combined. Increase
speed to medium; beat until mixture is smooth
and has changed to a paler colour. Divide
mixture into paper cases; smooth surface.
4 Bake about 25 minutes. Stand cakes in
pan 5 minutes; transfer to wire rack.
5 Meanwhile, make fruit mince filling.
6 Cut a 2cm (¾-inch) deep hole in the centre
of each warm cake; discard cake rounds. Fill
centres with fruit mixture, push in decorations;
dust with a little sifted icing sugar.
Christmas decorations On a surface dusted
with sifted icing sugar, knead icing until smooth;
roll out until 1cm (½ inch) thick. Cut out shapes
using Christmas cutters. Insert a length of damp
wire into each shape. Stand overnight on tray
lined with baking paper to dry.
fruit mince filling Warm fruit mince in small
saucepan over low heat; stir in icing sugar.

LITTLE CAKES
& PUDDINGS

FIG AND CRANBERRY FRUIT CAKES

prep + cook time **1 hour 10 minutes (+ cooling)**
makes **24**

60g (2 ounces) butter, softened
¼ cup (55g) firmly packed light brown sugar
1 egg
1 tablespoon orange marmalade
½ cup (80g) sultanas, chopped finely
½ cup (65g) dried cranberries,
    chopped finely
¼ cup (50g) finely chopped dried figs
¼ cup (40g) dried currants
⅓ cup (50g) plain (all-purpose) flour
2 tablespoons self-raising flour
½ teaspoon mixed spice
¼ cup (60ml) sweet sherry
1 tablespoon icing (confectioners') sugar
250g (8 ounces) ready-made white icing
2 tablespoons orange marmalade, warmed,
    strained, extra
24 edible sugar flowers

1 Preheat oven to 150°C/300°F. Line two
12-hole (1-tablespoon/20ml) mini muffin pans
with paper cases.
2 Beat butter, sugar and egg in small bowl with
electric mixer until combined. Stir in marmalade
and fruit, then sifted flours and spice with half
the sherry. Divide mixture into paper cases.
3 Bake cakes about 35 minutes. Remove
cakes from oven; brush tops with the remaining
sherry. Cover pans tightly with foil; cool cakes
in pans.
4 On surface dusted with sifted icing sugar,
knead white icing until smooth; roll out until
5mm (¼ inch) thick. Cut out 24 x 4cm (1½-inch)
fluted rounds from icing. Brush cold cakes with
extra marmalade; top with icing rounds. Brush
the bases of the sugar flowers with a little
water, push gently into icing.

rocky road Christmas tree cakes

ROCKY ROAD CHRISTMAS TREE CAKES

prep + cook time **1 hour 25 minutes**
(+ cooling & refrigeration) makes **4**

75g (2½ ounces) unsalted butter,
  chopped coarsely
75g (2½ ounces) white eating chocolate,
  chopped coarsely
⅓ cup (75g) caster (superfine) sugar
⅓ cup (80ml) milk
⅓ cup (50g) plain (all-purpose) flour
¼ cup (35g) self-raising flour
1 egg
rocky road
100g (3 ounces) toasted marshmallows with
  coconut, cut into 1cm (½-inch) pieces
200g (6½ ounces) turkish delight,
  chopped coarsely
½ cup (70g) roasted unsalted pistachios
450g (14½ ounces) white eating
  chocolate, melted

1 Preheat oven to 160°C/325°F. Grease
8cm x 26cm (3¼-inch x 10½-inch) bar cake
pan; line base and sides with baking paper,
extending paper 5cm (2 inches) over sides.
2 Combine butter, chocolate, sugar and milk in
small saucepan; stir over low heat until smooth.
Transfer to medium bowl; cool 10 minutes.
Whisk flours, then egg, into chocolate mixture.
Spread mixture into pan; bake about 45 minutes,
cool in pan.
3 Trim top of cake to make flat; cut four 4.5cm
(1¾-inch) rounds from cake. Chop cake scraps
into 1cm (½-inch) pieces; reserve.
4 Cut four 30cm (12-inch) circles from baking
paper. Fold each circle in half, then roll into a
cone shape, making sure the point of cone is
closed tightly. Staple or tape cone securely to
hold its shape.
5 Make rocky road. Spoon into cones; press
down firmly to pack tightly. Press one cake
round into base of each cone for a tree stump.
Stand each cone upright in a tall narrow glass.
Refrigerate about 1 hour or until set.
6 Remove paper from trees; serve upright.
rocky road Combine marshmallow, turkish
delight, nuts and reserved chopped cake in
large bowl; stir in chocolate.

fruit mince friands

FRUIT MINCE FRIANDS

prep + cook time **35 minutes** makes **12**

6 egg whites
185g (6 ounces) unsalted butter, melted
1 teaspoon finely grated orange rind
1 cup (120g) ground almonds
1½ cups (240g) icing (confectioners') sugar
½ cup (75g) plain (all-purpose) flour
½ cup (125g) fruit mince

1 Preheat oven to 180°C/350°F. Grease
12-hole (½-cup/125ml) oval friand pan.
2 Whisk egg whites in medium bowl until
frothy. Stir in butter, rind, almonds, then sifted
icing sugar and flour.
3 Spoon mixture into pan holes; bake friands
10 minutes. Remove friands from oven; press a
small, 1cm (½-inch) deep hole in top of each
friand with the end of a wooden spoon.
Spoon fruit mince into holes; bake friands
about 10 minutes.
4 Stand friands in pans 5 minutes; transfer
to wire rack to cool. Serve dusted with sifted
icing sugar.

MINI CHOCOLATE YULE LOGS

prep + cook time **1 hour 20 minutes**
(+ refrigeration & cooling) makes **4**

1 cup (150g) seeded dried dates
1 cup (190g) seeded prunes
1 cup (200g) dried figs
1 cup (140g) brazil nuts
2 eggs
½ cup (110g) firmly packed light brown sugar
1 tablespoon dark rum
100g (3 ounces) butter, melted
⅓ cup (50g) plain (all-purpose) flour
¼ cup (35g) self-raising flour
100g (3 ounces) dark eating (semi-sweet) chocolate, melted
1 tablespoon icing (confectioners') sugar
chocolate ganache
200g (6½ ounces) dark eating (semi-sweet) chocolate, chopped coarsely
½ cup (125ml) pouring cream

1 Preheat oven to 150°C/300°F. Grease cans (see tip); line with baking paper.
2 Chop fruit and nuts finely; combine in large bowl.
3 Beat eggs and sugar in small bowl with electric mixer until thick and creamy. Add rum, butter and sifted flours; beat until combined. Stir egg mixture into fruit mixture. Push mixture firmly into cans; place cans on oven tray.

4 Bake cakes about 30 minutes. Turn top-side up onto wire rack to cool.
5 Meanwhile, make chocolate ganache.
6 Line tray with baking paper; spread chocolate into a 26cm (10½-inch) square. Refrigerate until set.
7 Cut four cakes in half crossways. Sandwich one of the whole cakes and one of the half cakes, end-to-end, with ganache. Repeat with remaining whole cakes and three half cakes to make a total of four logs.
8 Trim bottom corner from each of the remaining cake halves at an angle. Attach to sides of long cakes with ganache to make log shapes.
9 Place logs on boards or serving plates; spread all over with ganache. Break chocolate into small pieces, gently push into ganache. Refrigerate until set. Serve dusted with sifted icing sugar.

chocolate ganache Stir ingredients in small bowl over small saucepan of simmering water until smooth. Refrigerate about 30 minutes, stirring occasionally, until spreadable.

tip We baked these cakes in eight 170g (5½-ounce) passionfruit pulp cans (5.5cm/2¼-inch diameter, 8.5cm/3½-inch tall). Open the cans with an opener that removes the rims from cans (ring-pull cans are not suitable). Freeze pulp for another use. Remove and discard the paper label from cans, then wash and dry the cans well.

SILVER STAR CUPCAKES

prep + cook time 1 hour 30 minutes (+ cooling)
makes 12

90g (3 ounces) butter, softened
½ cup (110g) firmly packed light brown sugar
2 eggs
1 tablespoon orange marmalade
500g (2¾ cups) mixed dried fruit,
    chopped finely
⅔ cup (100g) plain (all-purpose) flour
2 tablespoons self-raising flour
1 teaspoon mixed spice
⅓ cup (80ml) sweet sherry
½ cup (80g) icing (confectioners') sugar
315g (10 ounces) ready-made white icing
⅓ cup (110g) apricot jam, warmed, strained
½ teaspoon silver lustre (see tips)
½ teaspoon vodka
silver cachous

1 Preheat oven to 150°C/300°F. Line 12-hole (⅓-cup/80ml) muffin pan with paper cases.
2 Beat butter, sugar and eggs in small bowl with electric mixer until just combined. Stir in marmalade and fruit; mix well.
3 Sift flours and spice over mixture; add half the sherry, mix well. Divide mixture into paper cases; smooth surface.
4 Bake about 50 minutes. Remove from oven; brush tops with remaining sherry. Cover pan with foil; cool cakes in pan overnight.
5 On surface dusted with sifted icing sugar, knead white icing until smooth; roll out until 5mm (¼ inch) thick. Cut out 5.5cm (2¼-inch) rounds from icing.
6 Using a 2.5cm (1-inch) star-shaped cutter, gently press a star imprint into the centre of each icing round.
7 Brush cake tops with jam; top with icing rounds. Blend lustre with vodka; paint onto star imprints. Push silver cachous gently into rounds.

tips Silver lustre is a shimmer dust that gives a slight sparkle and helps create a wet look. It is available from cake decorating supply stores in 5g (¼ ounce) screw-top pots. This recipe also makes 6 texas muffins (¾-cup/180ml); bake about 1 hour.

MINI CHRISTMAS PUDDINGS

prep + cook time **4 hours 50 minutes (+ standing)**
makes **6**

1 cup (150g) raisins, chopped coarsely
1 cup (160g) sultanas
1 cup (150g) finely chopped seeded
    dried dates
½ cup (95g) finely chopped seeded prunes
½ cup (125g) finely chopped glacé apricots
½ cup (85g) mixed peel
1 teaspoon finely grated lemon rind
2 tablespoons lemon juice
2 tablespoons apricot jam
2 tablespoons brandy
250g (8 ounces) butter, softened
2 cups (440g) firmly packed light brown sugar
5 eggs
1¼ cups (185g) plain (all-purpose) flour
½ teaspoon each ground nutmeg and
    mixed spice
4 cups (280g) stale breadcrumbs
1 cup (150g) plain (all-purpose) flour, extra
6 x 30cm (12-inch) squares
    unbleached calico

1 Combine fruit, mixed peel, rind, juice, jam and brandy in large bowl. Cover; stand in cool, dark place for one week, stirring every day.
2 Beat butter and sugar in small bowl with electric mixer until combined; beat in eggs, one at a time. Stir butter mixture into fruit mixture. Stir in sifted dry ingredients and breadcrumbs.
3 Fill boiler three-quarters full of hot water, cover with tight lid; bring to the boil. Have ready 1m (3 feet) of kitchen string, plus extra flour. Wearing thick rubber gloves, dip pudding cloths, one at a time, into boiling water; boil 1 minute, then remove. Squeeze excess water from cloth. Spread hot cloths on bench; rub 2 tablespoons of the extra flour into centre of each cloth to cover an area about 18cm (7 inches) in diameter, leaving flour a little thicker in centre of cloth where "skin" on the pudding needs to be thickest.

4 Divide pudding mixture equally among cloths; placing in centre of each cloth. Gather cloths around mixture, avoiding any deep pleats; pat into round shapes. Tie cloths tightly with string, as close to mixture as possible. Tie loops in string. Lower three puddings into the boiling water. Cover; boil 2 hours, replenishing with boiling water as necessary to maintain water level.
5 Lift puddings from water, one at a time, using wooden spoons through string loops. Do not put pudding on bench; suspend from spoon by placing over rungs of upturned stool or wedging the spoon in a drawer. Twist ends of cloth around string to avoid them touching pudding; hang 10 minutes. Repeat with remaining puddings.
6 Place puddings on board; cut string, carefully peel back cloth. Turn puddings onto plates, then carefully peel cloth away completely. Stand at least 20 minutes or until skin darkens and pudding becomes firm.

tips **This recipe makes six generous single servings. You need six 30cm (12-inch) squares of unbleached calico for each pudding cloth. If the calico has not been used before, soak it in cold water overnight; the next day, boil it for 20 minutes, then rinse in cold water. Puddings can be cooked in two boilers or in batches; the mixture will keep at room temperature for several hours. Top puddings with a slice of glacé orange, if you like. It is available from gourmet and health-food stores. If you are giving the puddings as gifts, hang the puddings in their cloths until cold; they can be stored, in the refrigerator, for up to two months, or frozen for up to 12 months. To reheat puddings, lower clothed puddings into boiling water and boil, for about 1 hour, following instructions in steps 4 and 5. To reheat whole puddings in the microwave, cover unclothed pudding in plastic wrap and microwave on MEDIUM (55%) about 5 minutes or until hot. To reheat slices of leftover pudding, cover slices in plastic wrap and microwave on HIGH (100%) up to 1 minute per serve.**

TROPICAL FRUIT CAKES

prep + cook time **2 hours (+ cooling)** makes **6**

8 slices glacé pineapple (345g)
1 cup (180g) dried papaya
½ cup (90g) dried mango
½ cup (115g) glacé ginger
1 cup (140g) macadamia nuts
1 cup (170g) brazil nuts
2 eggs
½ cup (110g) firmly packed light brown sugar
1 tablespoon coconut-flavoured liqueur
100g (3 ounces) butter, melted
⅓ cup (50g) plain (all-purpose) flour
¼ cup (35g) self-raising flour
¼ cup (80g) apricot jam, warmed, strained
fruit and nut topping
3 slices glacé pineapple (170g)
¾ cup (135g) dried papaya
¼ cup (55g) glacé ginger
⅓ cup (45g) macadamia nuts
⅓ cup (55g) brazil nuts
½ cup (25g) coarsely grated fresh coconut

1 Preheat oven to 150°C/300°F. Grease six deep 8cm (3¼-inch) round cake pans; line with baking paper.

2 Coarsely chop fruit. Combine fruit and nuts in large bowl.

3 Beat eggs and sugar in small bowl with electric mixer until thick and creamy. Add liqueur, butter and sifted flours; beat until combined. Stir egg mixture into fruit mixture. Press mixture firmly into pans.

4 Make fruit and nut topping.

5 Gently press topping evenly over cake mixture; bake about 1¾ hours.

6 Turn cakes, top-side up, onto wire rack; brush tops with jam. Cool.

fruit and nut topping Coarsely chop fruit; combine with nuts and coconut in medium bowl.

tips Cover cakes with foil halfway through baking time if fruit on top starts to brown. We used Malibu for this recipe. You can buy flaked coconut from the supermarkets and use instead of the fresh coconut, if you prefer.

SPICED YO-YOS
WITH BRANDY BUTTER

prep + cook time 40 minutes (+ cooling) makes 32

250g (8 ounces) unsalted butter, softened
½ cup (110g) firmly packed dark brown sugar
1½ cups (225g) plain (all-purpose) flour
½ cup (75g) cornflour (cornstarch)
2 teaspoons ground ginger
1 teaspoon mixed spice
¼ teaspoon ground cloves
brandy butter
100g (3 ounces) unsalted butter, softened
⅔ cup (110g) icing (confectioners') sugar
2 tablespoons brandy

1 Preheat oven to 160°C/325°F. Grease oven
trays; line with baking paper.
2 Beat butter and sugar in small bowl with
electric mixer until light and fluffy; stir in sifted
dry ingredients, in two batches.
3 Roll rounded teaspoons of mixture into
balls. Place 3cm (1¼ inches) apart on trays;
flatten slightly using back of a fork. Bake
about 15 minutes; cool on trays.
4 Meanwhile, make brandy butter.
5 Sandwich biscuits with brandy butter.
brandy butter Beat butter and sifted icing
sugar in small bowl with electric mixer until light
and fluffy. Beat in brandy until combined.

tips Regular light brown sugar can be used instead of
dark brown sugar. Unfilled yo-yos will keep well for
about a week in an airtight container. Once filled, the
yo-yos will keep in the refrigerator for a few days.

BISCUITS & SLICES

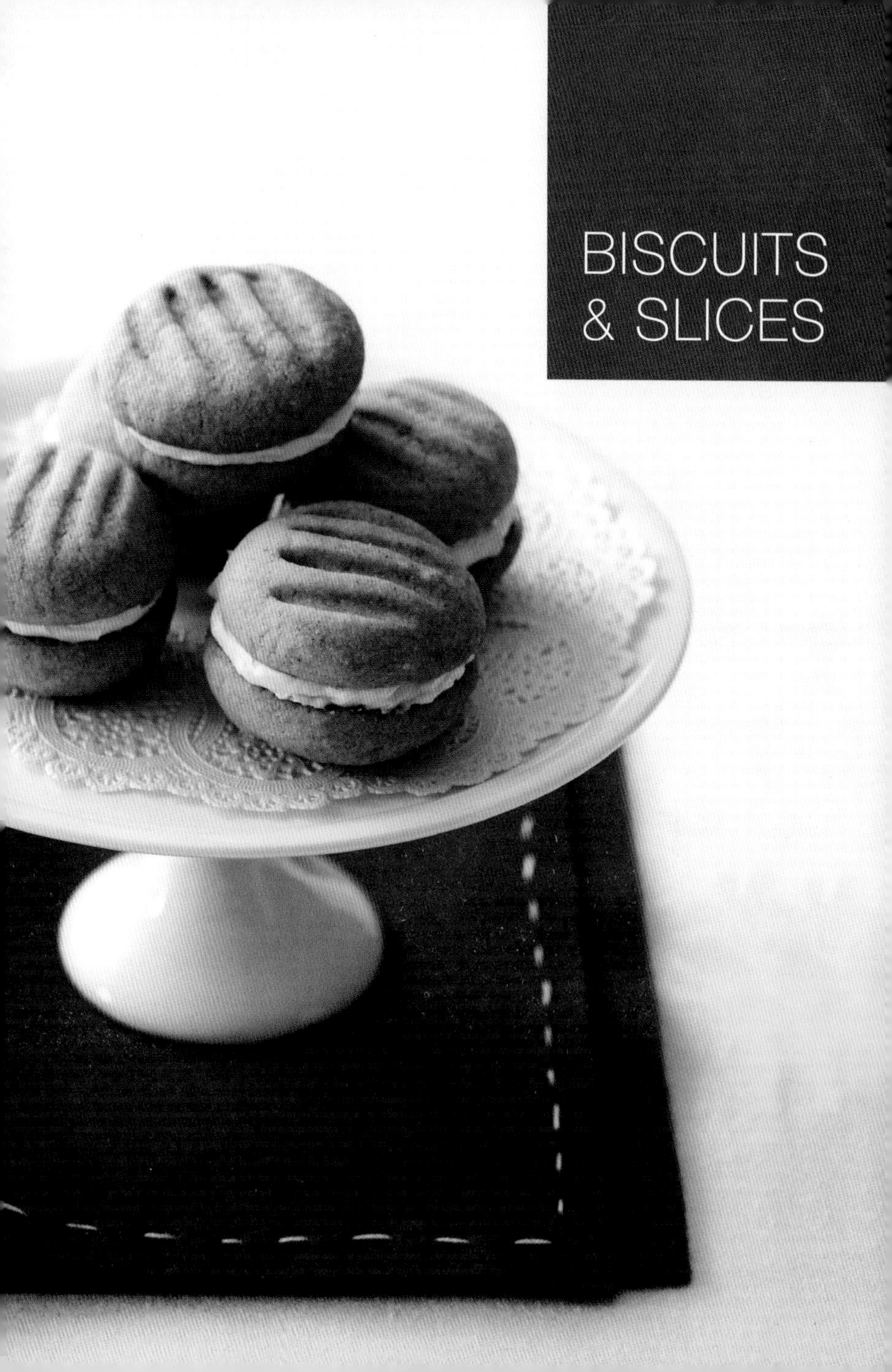

CHRISTMAS ANGELS

prep + cook time **50 minutes (+ refrigeration)** makes **16**

125g (4 ounces) butter, softened
¾ cup (165g) caster (superfine) sugar
1 egg
1½ cups (225g) plain (all-purpose) flour
¼ cup (35g) self-raising flour
½ cup (40g) desiccated coconut
⅓ cup (110g) apricot jam, warmed, strained
macaroon topping
3 egg whites
¾ cup (165g) caster (superfine) sugar
¼ cup (35g) plain (all-purpose) flour
2¼ cups (180g) desiccated coconut

1 Beat butter, sugar and egg in small bowl with electric mixer until light and fluffy. Stir in sifted flours and coconut, in two batches.

2 Knead dough on floured surface until smooth; roll dough between sheets of baking paper until 5mm (¼ inch) thick. Cover; refrigerate 30 minutes.

3 Preheat oven to 180°C/350°F. Grease oven trays; line with baking paper.

4 Make macaroon topping.

5 Cut 16 x 11cm (4½-inch) angel shapes from dough. Place, about 3cm (1¼ inches) apart, on oven trays.

6 Bake 8 minutes. Spread each hot cookie with jam; divide macaroon topping onto angels. Cover with foil (like a tent so foil does not touch surface of macaroon). Bake about 7 minutes. Cool on wire racks.

macaroon topping Beat egg whites in small bowl with electric mixer until soft peaks form. Gradually add sugar, beating until sugar dissolves. Fold in sifted flour and coconut, in two batches.

Christmas pudding cookies

CHRISTMAS PUDDING COOKIES

prep + cook time **45 minutes**
(+ refrigeration, cooling & standing) makes **30**

1⅔ cups (250g) plain (all-purpose) flour
⅓ cup (40g) ground almonds
⅓ cup (75g) caster (superfine) sugar
1 teaspoon mixed spice
1 teaspoon vanilla extract
125g (4 ounces) cold butter,
   chopped coarsely
2 tablespoons water
700g (1½ pounds) rich dark fruit cake
⅓ cup (80ml) brandy
1 egg white, beaten lightly
400g (12½ ounces) dark eating (semi-sweet)
   chocolate, melted
½ cup (75g) white chocolate Melts, melted
30 red glacé cherries

1 Process flour, almonds, sugar, spice, extract
and butter until crumbly. Add the water, process
until ingredients come together.
2 Knead dough on floured surface until
smooth; roll dough between sheets of baking
paper until 5mm (¼ inch) thick. Cover;
refrigerate 30 minutes.
3 Preheat oven to 180°C/350°F. Grease oven
trays; line with baking paper.
4 Cut 30 x 5.5cm (2¼-inch) rounds from
dough. Place about 3cm (1¼ inches) apart on
oven trays. Bake about 10 minutes.
5 Meanwhile, crumble fruit cake into a medium
bowl; add brandy. Press mixture firmly into
round metal tablespoon measures. Brush
partially baked cookies with egg white, top with
cake domes; bake further 5 minutes. Cool on
wire racks.
6 Place wire racks over oven tray, coat cookies
with dark chocolate. Set at room temperature.
7 Spoon white chocolate over cookies; top
with cherries. Set at room temperature.

frozen jaffa slice

FROZEN JAFFA SLICE

prep + cook time **1 hour** (+ freezing) makes **64**

4 eggs
⅓ cup (75g) firmly packed light brown sugar
300g (9½ ounces) dark eating (semi-sweet)
   chocolate, melted
300g (9½ ounces) thick (double)
   cream (48% fat)
¼ cup (60ml) orange-flavoured liqueur
3 slices glacé orange (60g), chopped finely

1 Preheat oven to 180°C/350°F. Grease deep
22cm (9-inch) square cake pan; line base and
sides with baking paper.
2 Beat eggs and sugar in small bowl with
electric mixer until thick and creamy. Beat in
cooled chocolate until combined.
3 Fold in combined cream, liqueur and orange;
pour mixture into pan. Place pan in baking
dish; pour enough boiling water into dish to
come halfway up side of pan. Bake about
35 minutes or until slice is barely set; cool slice
in pan. Cover; freeze overnight.
4 Remove frozen slice from pan; stand at
room temperature 10 minutes. Cut into squares
to serve.

hazelnut shortbread trees

HAZELNUT SHORTBREAD TREES

prep + cook time **45 minutes (+ refrigeration)** makes **12**

250g (8 ounces) butter, softened
2 teaspoons finely grated orange rind
½ cup (80g) icing (confectioners') sugar
2 tablespoons rice flour
2 cups (300g) plain (all-purpose) flour
2 teaspoons mixed spice
¼ cup (25g) ground hazelnuts
silver cachous
1 tablespoon icing (confectioners') sugar, extra
brandy butter cream
60g (2 ounces) butter, softened
½ teaspoon finely grated orange rind
¾ cup (120g) icing (confectioners') sugar
2 teaspoons brandy

1 Beat butter, rind and sifted icing sugar in small bowl with electric mixer until light and fluffy. Transfer to large bowl. Stir in sifted flours, spice and hazelnuts, in two batches.
2 Knead dough on floured surface until smooth. Roll dough between sheets of baking paper until 5mm (¼ inch) thick; refrigerate 30 minutes.

3 Preheat oven to 180°C/350°F. Grease three oven trays; line with baking paper.
4 Cut 24 x 3cm (1¼-inch) stars, 24 x 5cm (2-inch) stars and 24 x 7cm (2¾-inch) stars from dough. Place small stars, about 1cm (½ inch) apart, on an oven tray; place remaining stars, about 2cm (¾ inch) apart, on oven trays.
5 Bake small stars about 10 minutes. Bake larger stars about 15 minutes. Stand cookies on trays 5 minutes; transfer to wire racks to cool.
6 Meanwhile, make brandy butter cream.
7 Sandwich two of each sized cookie with butter cream. Assemble trees by joining three different sized stars together with butter cream.
8 Decorate trees by joining cachous to stars with a tiny dot of butter cream. Dust trees with extra sifted icing sugar.
brandy butter cream Beat butter, rind, sifted icing sugar and brandy in small bowl with electric mixer until light and fluffy.

STAINED GLASS BISCOTTI

prep + cook time **1 hour 25 minutes** makes **60**

¾ cup (165g) caster (superfine) sugar
2 eggs
1⅓ cups (200g) plain (all-purpose) flour
⅓ cup (50g) self-raising flour
1½ cups (300g) multi glacé cherries (a mix of yellow, green and red cherries), halved
½ cup (80g) blanched almonds

1 Preheat oven to 180°C/350°F. Grease oven tray.
2 Whisk sugar and eggs in medium bowl until combined; stir in sifted flours then cherries and nuts.
3 Knead dough on floured surface until smooth. Divide dough in half, roll each portion into a 30cm (12-inch) log; place logs on tray. Bake about 30 minutes. Cool on tray 10 minutes.
4 Reduce oven temperature to 150°C/300°F.
5 Using serrated knife, cut logs diagonally into 5mm (¼-inch) slices. Place slices, in single layer, on ungreased oven trays. Bake biscotti about 30 minutes or until dry and crisp, turning halfway through baking. Cool on wire racks.

stained glass biscotti

fig and muscat brownies

FIG AND MUSCAT BROWNIES

prep + cook time **45 minutes** (+ standing & cooling)
makes **36**

½ cup (100g) finely chopped dried figs
¼ cup (60ml) muscat
125g (4 ounces) butter, chopped coarsely
200g (6½ ounces) dark eating (semi-sweet)
    chocolate, chopped coarsely
⅔ cup (150g) caster (superfine) sugar
2 eggs, beaten lightly
1¼ cups (185g) plain (all-purpose) flour
150g (4½ ounces) dark eating (semi-sweet)
    chocolate, chopped coarsely, extra
1 tablespoon cocoa powder

1 Combine figs and muscat in small bowl;
stand 20 minutes.
2 Preheat oven to 180°C/350°F. Grease deep
20cm (8-inch) square cake pan; line base and
sides with baking paper, extending paper 5cm
(2 inches) over sides.
3 Stir butter and chocolate in medium
saucepan over low heat until smooth. Cool
10 minutes.
4 Stir in sugar and eggs then sifted flour,
extra chocolate and fig mixture. Spread mixture
into pan.
5 Bake brownies about 30 minutes. Cool in pan.
6 Dust brownies with sifted cocoa; cut into
squares to serve.

JAM WREATHS

prep + cook time **45 minutes** (+ refrigeration) makes **20**

250g (8 ounces) butter, softened
1 teaspoon finely grated lemon rind
⅓ cup (75g) caster (superfine) sugar
2 cups (300g) plain (all-purpose) flour
½ cup (100g) rice flour
1 tablespoon caster (superfine) sugar, extra
½ cup (160g) raspberry jam

jam wreaths

1 Beat butter, rind and sugar in medium bowl
with electric mixer until combined. Stir in sifted
flours, in two batches. Knead dough on floured
surface until smooth. Wrap dough in plastic;
refrigerate 30 minutes.
2 Preheat oven to 180°C/350°F. Line two oven
trays with baking paper.
3 Roll three-quarters of the dough between
sheets of baking paper until 3mm (⅛ inch)
thick; cut 20 x 6.5cm (2¾-inch) rounds from
dough. Place rounds 4cm (1½ inches) apart on
oven trays.
4 Roll remaining dough between sheets of
baking paper until 3mm (⅛ inch) thick. Using a
4cm (1½-inch) holly cutter, cut out leaves from
dough.
5 Brush edge of each round of dough lightly
with water; arrange leaves, overlapping
slightly, around edge. Sprinkle leaves lightly
with extra sugar. Spoon jam into the centre
of each wreath.
6 Bake wreaths about 20 minutes. Cool
on trays.

MINI GINGERBREAD HOUSES

prep + cook time **2 hours 30 minutes**
(+ refrigeration, cooling & standing) makes **4**

3 cups (450g) self-raising flour
¾ cup (165g) firmly packed light brown sugar
1 tablespoon ground ginger
1 teaspoon each ground cinnamon
  and nutmeg
½ teaspoon ground cloves
185g (6 ounces) butter, softened
¾ cup (270g) golden syrup or treacle
1 egg
1 cup (70g) All-Bran
silver cachous
assorted lollies
2 tablespoons pure icing (confectioners') sugar
royal icing
3 cups (480g) pure icing (confectioners')
  sugar, approximately
2 egg whites

1 Process flour, sugar, spices and butter until mixture is crumbly. Add syrup and egg; process until combined. Knead dough on floured surface until smooth. Wrap dough in plastic; refrigerate 1 hour.
2 Meanwhile, cut out paper patterns for gingerbread houses. Cut two 7cm x 9cm (2¾-inch x 3¾-inch) rectangles for roof; two 6cm (2½-inch) squares for side walls, and two 7cm x 9cm (2¾-inch x 3¾-inch) rectangles for front and back walls. Trim front and back walls to form two 6cm (2½-inch) high gables.

3 Preheat oven to 180°C/350°F. Roll dough between sheets of baking paper until 5mm (¼ inch) thick. Peel away top paper; use patterns to cut shapes from dough. Pull away excess dough around shapes; slide baking paper with shapes onto oven trays. Bake about 12 minutes or until shapes are slightly firm.
4 While shapes are still warm and soft, use tip of sharp knife to trim all shapes to straighten sides; transfer shapes to wire rack to cool.
5 Make royal icing.
6 Assemble houses, securing roofs and walls together with icing. If possible, stand houses several hours or overnight, supporting sides with four cans, so that they are thoroughly dry before decorating. Spread royal icing onto roofs, decorate with All-Bran and cachous. Decorate houses with lollies, securing with royal icing. Dust house with a little sifted icing sugar.
royal icing Sift icing sugar through fine sieve. Lightly beat egg whites in small bowl with electric mixer; beat in icing sugar, a tablespoon at a time. Continue beating until icing reaches firm peaks; cover tightly with plastic wrap until ready to use.

mini gingerbread houses

jammy spice drops

JAMMY SPICE DROPS

prep + cook time **45 minutes**
(+ cooling & standing) makes **24**

30g (1 ounce) butter
⅓ cup (115g) golden syrup or treacle
1 cup (150g) plain (all-purpose) flour
½ teaspoon bicarbonate of soda (baking soda)
¼ teaspoon each ground ginger, cardamom,
    cinnamon and cloves
½ teaspoon cocoa powder
1 tablespoon milk
2 tablespoons finely chopped mixed peel
¼ cup (80g) raspberry jam
60g (2 ounces) dark eating (semi-sweet)
    chocolate, melted

1 Melt butter in small saucepan; add syrup,
bring to the boil. Remove from heat; stand
10 minutes.
2 Stir in sifted dry ingredients, milk and peel.
Cover; cool 2 hours.
3 Preheat oven to 180°C/350°F. Grease two
oven trays.
4 Knead dough on floured surface until dough
loses stickiness.
5 Roll dough between sheets of baking paper
until about 8mm (¼ inch) thick. Cut 24 x 4cm
(1½-inch) fluted rounds from dough. Place
about 3cm (1¼ inches) apart on trays.
6 Using end of handle of wooden spoon,
gently press hollows into each round; fill with
½ teaspoon jam.
7 Bake about 10 minutes; cool on trays.
8 Spread flat-sides of biscuits with chocolate.
Place biscuits, jam-side down, on foil-lined
trays; set at room temperature.

jewelled rocky road

JEWELLED ROCKY ROAD

prep time **25 minutes** (+ refrigeration) makes **35**

300g (9½ ounces) toasted marshmallows
    with coconut, chopped coarsely
½ cup (40g) flaked almonds, roasted
4 slices glacé pineapple (125g),
    chopped coarsely
½ cup (125g) coarsely chopped
    glacé peaches
½ cup (100g) coarsely chopped glacé citron
450g (14½ ounces) white eating
    chocolate, melted

1 Grease 20cm x 30cm (8-inch x 12-inch)
rectangular pan; line base and two long sides
with baking paper, extending paper 5cm
(2 inches) over long sides.
2 Combine marshmallows, nuts and fruit in
large bowl. Working quickly, stir in chocolate;
spread mixture into pan, push mixture down
firmly to flatten.
3 Refrigerate rocky road until set before cutting.

GINGERBREAD CHRISTMAS TREES

prep + cook time **1 hour 20 minutes**
(+ refrigeration & cooling) makes **6**

3 cups (450g) self-raising flour
¾ cup (165g) firmly packed light brown sugar
1 tablespoon ground ginger
1 teaspoon each ground cinnamon
   and nutmeg
½ teaspoon ground cloves
185g (6 ounces) butter, chopped coarsely
¾ cup (270g) golden syrup or treacle
1 egg
silver cachous
1 tablespoon pure icing (confectioners')
   sugar
royal icing
1 egg white
1½ cups (240g) pure icing (confectioners')
   sugar

1 Process flour, brown sugar, spices and butter until crumbly. Add golden syrup and egg; process until combined. Knead dough on floured surface until smooth. Wrap dough in plastic; refrigerate 1 hour.
2 Divide dough in half; roll each half between sheets of baking paper until 5mm (¼ inch) thick. Refrigerate 30 minutes.

3 Preheat oven to 180°C/350°F. Line oven trays with baking paper.
4 Cut 12 x 3cm (1¼-inch), 12 x 5cm (2-inch), 12 x 6cm (2¼-inch), 12 x 7cm (2¾-inch), 12 x 8cm (3¼-inch) and 12 x 9cm (3¾-inch) stars from dough; transfer stars to trays. You will need to reroll the dough several times to get the correct number of stars.
5 Bake 3cm, 5cm and 6cm stars about 10 minutes and remaining stars about 12 minutes. Cool on trays.
6 Meanwhile, make royal icing.
7 Assemble trees by joining each star with another same-sized star using a little royal icing. Ensure the points of the stars alternate. Still using royal icing to join, stack different-sized paired stars on top of one another, largest to smallest, to form six trees. Decorate trees by joining cachous to stars with a tiny dot of royal icing. Dust trees with sifted icing sugar.
royal icing Sift icing sugar through fine sieve. Beat egg white until foamy in small bowl with electric mixer; beat in icing sugar, a tablespoon at a time. Continue beating until icing reaches firm peaks; cover tightly with plastic wrap until ready to use.

tips **The trees will keep for several weeks in airtight containers. You will have a lot of royal icing left over; use it for making snow on the trees, if you like.**

LITTLE CHOCOLATE
CHRISTMAS PUDDINGS

prep + cook time 45 minutes (+ refrigeration & cooling)
makes 45

700g (1½-pound) plum pudding
250g (8 ounces) dark eating (semi-sweet)
    chocolate, melted
½ cup (125ml) brandy
½ cup (80g) icing (confectioners') sugar
200g (6½ ounces) white chocolate Melts
red and green glacé cherries, cut to
    resemble berries and leaves

1 Crumble pudding into large bowl. Stir in
melted chocolate, brandy and sifted icing
sugar; mix well.
2 Roll level tablespoons of mixture into balls;
place on baking-paper-lined tray. Cover;
refrigerate until firm.
3 Melt white chocolate in small heatproof bowl
over small saucepan of simmering water. Cool
chocolate 10 minutes. Drizzle over puddings to
form "custard"; decorate with cherries.

tips You can use either bought or leftover homemade
pudding. This recipe can be made two weeks ahead.

CHOCOLATES
& SWEETS

ALMOND HONEY NOUGAT

prep + cook time **40 minutes (+ standing)** makes **49**

2 sheets edible rice paper
½ cup (175g) honey
1⅓ cups (295g) caster (superfine) sugar
2 tablespoons water
1 egg white
2 cups (320g) blanched almonds, roasted

1 Grease deep 15cm (6-inch) square cake pan. Trim one sheet of rice paper to fit base of pan.

2 Combine honey, sugar and the water in small heavy-based saucepan with pouring lip; stir over heat, without boiling, until sugar dissolves. Bring to the boil; boil, uncovered, without stirring, about 10 minutes or until syrup reaches 164°C/325°F on the candy thermometer. Remove pan from heat immediately; remove thermometer from pan.

3 Beat egg white in small heatproof bowl with electric mixer until soft peaks form. With motor operating, add hot syrup to egg white in thin, steady stream.

4 Working quickly, stir nuts into egg white mixture; spoon into pan. Press mixture firmly into pan. Cut remaining sheet of rice paper large enough to cover top of nougat; press gently onto nougat. Stand at room temperature about 2 hours or until cool, before cutting.

tips It is important to use a candy thermometer in this recipe in order to get the correct consistency when making the nougat. Rice paper, used for confectionery, can be found in specialist food stores and some delis. Store cut nougat, at room temperature, in an airtight container.

jewelled macaroons

JEWELLED MACAROONS

prep + cook time **45 minutes (+ cooling)** makes **24**

1 egg white
¼ cup (55g) caster (superfine) sugar
¾ cup (60g) shredded coconut
2 tablespoons each finely chopped glacé
   apricot, glacé pineapple, glacé red
      cherries and glacé green cherries
2 tablespoons finely chopped roasted,
   unsalted pistachios

1 Preheat oven to 150°C/300°F. Line two
12-hole (1-tablespoon/20ml) mini muffin pans
with paper cases.
2 Beat egg white in small bowl with electric
mixer until soft peaks form; gradually add
sugar, beating until sugar dissolves. Fold
coconut and half the combined fruit and nuts
into egg white mixture.
3 Divide mixture between paper cases.
Sprinkle with remaining fruit and nut mixture.
Bake about 20 minutes; cool macaroons
in pans.

tips Cover macaroons with foil halfway through baking
time if fruit on top starts to brown. You need
approximately 50g (1½ ounces) of each glacé fruit.

SIENNA DISCS

prep + cook time **1 hour 30 minutes**
(+ cooling & standing) makes **30**

2 tablespoons caster (superfine) sugar
¼ cup (90g) honey
⅓ cup (55g) blanched almonds, roasted
½ cup (70g) roasted hazelnuts
1 glacé apricot (30g)
1 slice glacé pineapple (30g)
2 tablespoons mixed peel
⅓ cup (50g) plain (all-purpose) flour
1 tablespoon cocoa powder
½ teaspoon ground cinnamon
30g (1 ounce) dark eating (semi-sweet)
   chocolate, melted
100g (3 ounces) dark eating (semi-sweet)
   chocolate, melted, extra

sienna discs

1 Preheat oven to 160°C/325°F. Grease 40cm
(16-inch) long strip of foil.
2 Combine sugar and honey in small
saucepan; stir over heat, without boiling, until
sugar dissolves. Bring to a simmer; simmer,
uncovered, without stirring, until syrup thickens
slightly. Remove pan from heat.
3 Meanwhile, chop nuts, fruit and peel finely;
combine mixture in medium bowl with syrup.
4 Stir in sifted flour, cocoa and cinnamon,
then chocolate.
5 Shape mixture into 5cm (2-inch) diameter
log; roll tightly in foil, place on oven tray.
6 Bake 45 minutes; remove foil, cool on tray
overnight.
7 Slice log; place slices on wire racks, pipe or
drizzle extra chocolate over slices. Set at room
temperature.

CHRISTMAS ICE-CREAM PUDDING BITES

prep + cook time **20 minutes (+ freezing)** makes **28**

2 cups (500ml) vanilla ice-cream, softened
1 cup (200g) christmas pudding,
chopped finely
400g (12½ ounces) dark eating (semi-sweet)
chocolate, chopped coarsely

1 Grease two 14-hole ice-cube trays. Line small oven tray with baking paper. Place 28 mini muffin paper cases on another small tray.
2 Working quickly, combine ice-cream and pudding in medium bowl; press mixture into ice-cube tray holes. Freeze about 2 hours or until firm. Unmould bites onto tray; freeze 30 minutes.

3 Meanwhile, melt half the chocolate in medium heatproof bowl over medium saucepan of simmering water. Remove from heat; stand 5 minutes.
4 Working quickly and using small cocktail toothpicks, dip half the ice-cream blocks, one at a time, into chocolate until covered; place on baking-paper-covered tray. Freeze until ready to serve.
5 Repeat melting and dipping with remaining chocolate and ice-cream blocks; freeze until ready to serve. Serve bites in paper cases.

tips **These little morsels only improve with time. Make 1 or 2 days ahead. Use rounded ice-cube trays if possible as the ice-cream blocks will unmould more easily. You can also make this as a log. Place ice-cream mixture in a bar cake pan lined with baking paper. Once frozen, place on a wire rack and drizzle with melted chocolate to cover. Transfer to a serving plate; freeze until ready to serve.**

caramel nut chocolates

CARAMEL NUT CHOCOLATES

prep + cook time **55 minutes**
(+ cooling & refrigeration) makes **32**

60g (2 ounces) butter
½ cup (110g) caster (superfine) sugar
1 tablespoon golden syrup or treacle
¾ cup (250g) sweetened condensed milk
½ teaspoon vanilla extract
½ cup (75g) unsalted peanuts,
    chopped coarsely
¼ cup (25g) ground hazelnuts or almonds
100g (3 ounces) dark eating (semi-sweet)
    chocolate, chopped coarsely
1 teaspoon vegetable oil
50g (1½ ounces) dark eating (semi-sweet)
    chocolate, extra, melted

1 Combine butter, sugar and syrup in small saucepan; stir over heat, without boiling, until sugar dissolves. Stir in condensed milk; bring to the boil. Reduce heat; cook, stirring, about 6 minutes or until mixture turns a caramel colour. Remove from heat; stir in extract and nuts. Transfer mixture to medium heatproof bowl; cool 10 minutes.
2 Roll rounded teaspoons of mixture into balls; place on tray. Refrigerate until firm.
3 Combine chocolate and oil in medium heatproof bowl; stir over medium saucepan of simmering water until smooth. Dip balls in chocolate mixture using a fork or skewer. Lift balls from chocolate; allow excess chocolate to drip away. Place on tray lined with aluminium foil or baking paper. Refrigerate until set.
4 Drizzle extra melted chocolate over balls. Refrigerate until set.

tip **Refrigerate in an airtight container for up to one week.**

coconut christmas wreaths

COCONUT CHRISTMAS WREATHS

prep time **25 minutes** (+ refrigeration) makes **8**

180g (5½ ounces) white eating chocolate,
    melted
1¼ cups (95g) shredded coconut
silver cachous

1 Line two trays with baking paper.
2 Combine chocolate and coconut in medium bowl. Drop heaped tablespoons of mixture onto trays; shape mixture into wreaths using the end of a wooden spoon to make holes in the centre of each wreath.
3 Decorate wreaths with cachous. Refrigerate until set. Tie with ribbon, if you like.

TURKISH DELIGHT

prep + cook time **40 minutes**
(+ cooling & standing) makes **48**

¼ cup (45g) gelatine
¼ cup (60ml) water
3 cups (660g) caster (superfine) sugar
2 cups (500ml) water, extra
¾ cup (110g) wheaten cornflour (cornstarch)
2 tablespoons glucose syrup
¼ cup (60ml) rosewater
red food colouring
⅔ cup (110g) icing (confectioners') sugar

1 Grease deep 20cm (8-inch) square cake pan.
2 Sprinkle gelatine over the water in small jug; stand jug in small saucepan of simmering water. Stir until gelatine dissolves.
3 Combine caster sugar and ¾ cup of the extra water in medium saucepan; stir over low heat until sugar dissolves. Bring to the boil; boil, without stirring, until temperature of the syrup reaches 116°C/235°F (soft ball) on candy thermometer. Simmer at 116°C/235°F for 5 minutes, without stirring, regulating heat to maintain temperature at 116°C/235°F. Remove pan from heat.

4 Meanwhile, place cornflour in another medium saucepan; gradually blend in the remaining extra water. Bring to the boil, stirring, until mixture thickens.
5 Gradually stir hot sugar syrup, gelatine mixture and glucose into cornflour mixture; bring to the boil, stirring. Reduce heat; simmer, stirring, about 10 minutes or until mixture thickens a little more. Remove pan from heat; whisk in rosewater, tint with red food colouring.
6 Strain mixture through fine sieve into cake pan; skim any scum from surface. Stand 15 minutes; cover surface with lightly greased baking paper, stand overnight.
7 Turn turkish delight onto board dusted with sifted icing sugar, dust with more sifted icing sugar; cut with icing-sugar-coated knife. Roll pieces in remaining sifted icing sugar.

tips **You must use a candy thermometer to get the correct consistency for turkish delight. Store turkish delight in an airtight container at room temperature for up to two weeks.**

BROWNIE BOMBS

prep + cook time **1 hour (+ cooling)** makes **50**

Preheat oven to 180°C/350°F. Grease deep 20cm (8-inch) square cake pan; line base and sides with baking paper. Stir 125g (4 ounces) coarsely chopped butter and 200g (6½ ounces) coarsely chopped dark eating (semi-sweet) chocolate in medium saucepan over low heat until smooth; transfer to large bowl, cool 10 minutes. Stir in ⅔ cup caster (superfine) sugar, 2 lightly beaten eggs and 1¼ cups sifted plain (all-purpose) flour. Spread mixture into pan; bake about 30 minutes. Cool in pan. Cut cake into large pieces; process with ⅓ cup dark rum until mixture comes together. Roll heaped teaspoons of mixture into balls. Freeze for 10 minutes. Melt 200g (6½ ounces) coarsely chopped dark eating (semi-sweet) chocolate; dip balls in to coat. Refrigerate until set. Drizzle with 60g (2 ounces) melted white eating chocolate, top with pieces of red glacé cherry.

CHRISTMAS MUFFINS

prep + cook time **40 minutes** makes **12**

Preheat oven to 200°C/400°F. Grease 12-hole (⅓-cup/80ml) muffin pan. Sift 2½ cups self-raising flour into medium bowl; rub in 100g (3 ounces) coarsely chopped cold butter. Gently stir in 1 cup caster (superfine) sugar, 1¼ cups buttermilk and 1 beaten egg. Gently stir in 1 cup mixed coarsely chopped glacé fruit. Spoon mixture into pan holes; bake about 20 minutes. Stand muffins 5 minutes; transfer to wire rack to cool. Roll 250g (8 ounces) ready-made white icing out until 5mm (¼ inch) thick; cut out 12 x 4.5cm (1¾-inch) stars. Brush tops of muffins with 2 tablespoons warmed, strained apricot jam; top with icing stars. Dust with sifted icing (confectioners') sugar, if you like.

SWEET GIFTS

CHRISTMAS COOKIES

prep + cook time **30 minutes (+ refrigeration)** makes **28**

Grease oven trays; line with baking paper.
Beat 250g (8 ounces) softened butter, ¾ cup
caster (superfine) sugar and 1 egg in small
bowl with electric mixer until light and fluffy;
transfer to large bowl. Stir in 2¼ cups sifted
plain (all-purpose) flour. Knead dough on
floured surface until smooth; wrap dough in
plastic, refrigerate 30 minutes. Preheat oven
to 180°C/350°F. Roll heaped teaspoons of
mixture into 15cm (6-inch) log shapes. Twist
2 pieces of dough together, shape into canes
and wreaths. Place on trays. Bake about 12
minutes; cool cookies on trays. Sprinkle hot
cookies with 2 tablespoons cinnamon sugar.

FRUIT NUT CLUSTERS

prep + cook time **30 minutes (+ refrigeration)** makes **36**

Line three 12-hole (2-tablespoon/40ml) deep
flat-based patty pans with paper patty cases.
Stir 150g (4½ ounces) coarsely chopped
butter, ½ cup caster (superfine) sugar and
2 tablespoons honey in small saucepan over
low heat until sugar dissolves. Combine
3½ cups cornflakes, ½ cup coarsely chopped
dried cranberries, ½ cup roasted flaked
almonds, ½ cup coarsely chopped roasted
unsalted pistachios and ⅓ cup finely chopped
glacé peach in large bowl. Stir in butter
mixture. Spoon mixture into paper cases;
refrigerate until set.

ALMONDS flat, pointy-tipped nuts with a pitted brown shell enclosing a creamy white kernel which is covered by a brown skin.

blanched brown skins removed.

flaked paper-thin slices.

ground also known as almond meal.

BAKING POWDER a raising agent that aerates and lightens cake mixtures.

BICARBONATE OF SODA also known as baking or carb soda.

BREAD

french stick bread that's been formed into a long, narrow cylindrical loaf. Is also known as french bread, french loaf or baguette.

BREADCRUMBS

fresh bread, usually white, processed into crumbs.

stale one- or two-day-old bread made into crumbs by blending or processing.

BUTTER we use salted butter; 125g is equal to one stick (4 ounces) of butter.

unsalted often called 'sweet' butter; it simply has no added salt. It's advisable to stick to unsalted butter when it's called for in delicate recipes.

BUTTERMILK originally the term given to the slightly sour liquid left after butter was churned from cream, today it is commercially made similarly to yogurt. Sold alongside all fresh milk products in supermarkets. Despite the implication of its name, it's low in fat.

CACHOUS also called dragées in some countries; minuscule metallic-looking but edible confectionery balls used in cake decorating; available in silver, gold or various colours.

CAPERS the grey-green buds of a warm-climate (usually Mediterranean) shrub, sold either dried and salted or pickled in a vinegar brine. Tiny young ones, called baby capers, are also available both in brine or dried in salt. Capers must be rinsed well before using.

CAYENNE PEPPER a long, thin-fleshed, extremely hot red chilli usually sold dried and ground.

CHEESE

camembert soft-ripened cow's-milk cheese with a delicate, creamy texture and a rich, sweet-sharp taste that varies from buttery to mushroomy. Best served at room temperature after a brief period of ageing, camembert should have a bloomy white rind and voluptuous centre. Overripe camembert will have a runny bitter centre.

haloumi a firm, cream-coloured sheep's-milk cheese matured in brine; somewhat like a minty, salty fetta in flavour, haloumi can be grilled or fried, briefly, without breaking down. Should be eaten while still warm as it becomes tough and rubbery on cooling.

CHERVIL a herb also known as cicily.

CHOCOLATE

dark eating also known as semi-sweet or luxury chocolate; made of a high percentage of cocoa liquor and cocoa butter, and a little added sugar.

Melts small discs of compounded milk, white or dark chocolate ideal for melting and moulding.

white eating contains no cocoa solids but derives its sweet flavour from cocoa butter. Very sensitive to heat, so watch carefully if melting.

COCOA POWDER also known as cocoa; dried, unsweetened, roasted then ground cocoa beans (cacao seeds).

CORIANDER also known as pak chee, cilantro or chinese parsley; bright-green leafy herb with a pungent flavour. Also available ground or as seeds; these should not be substituted for fresh coriander as the tastes are completely different.

CORNFLOUR also known as cornstarch; used as a thickening agent. Available as 100% maize (corn) and as wheaten cornflour (wheaten has added gluten).

CORNICHONS French for gherkin, a very small variety of cucumber.

CRANBERRIES, DRIED have the same slightly sour, succulent flavour as fresh cranberries. Available in supermarkets.

CREAM we used fresh cream, also known as pure cream and pouring cream, unless otherwise stated; it has no additives unlike commercially thickened cream. Minimum fat content 35%.

sour a thick commercially-cultured soured cream. Minimum fat content 35%.

thick does not contain any thickening agents and usually has a fat content of around 48% or more.

thickened a whipping cream containing a thickener. Minimum fat content 35%.

crème fraîche mature fermented cream having a slightly tangy, nutty flavour and velvety texture. Minimum fat content 35%.

CUCUMBER, LEBANESE short, slender and thin-skinned. Has tender, edible skin, tiny seeds, and a sweet, fresh and flavoursome taste.

CUMIN also known as zeera or comino.

CURRANTS, DRIED tiny, almost black raisins so-named after a grape variety that originated in Corinth, Greece.

DUKKAH an Egyptian specialty spice mixture made up of roasted nuts, seeds and an array of aromatic spices.

EGGPLANT also known as aubergine.

FLOUR

plain all-purpose flour, made from wheat.

rice very fine flour, made from ground white rice.

self-raising also called self-rising, plain flour sifted with baking powder in the proportion of 1 cup flour to 2 teaspoons baking powder.

spelt very similar to wheaten flour, but has a slightly nuttier, sweeter flavour. Available from health-food stores.

FRUIT MINCE also known as mincemeat. A mixture of dried fruits such as raisins, sultanas and candied peel, nuts, spices, apple, brandy or rum. Is used as a filling for cakes, puddings and fruit mince pies.

GELATINE we use dried (powdered) gelatine in this book; it's also available in sheet form known as leaf gelatine. A thickening agent made from either collagen, a protein found in animal connective tissue and bones, or certain algae (agar-agar). Three teaspoons of dried gelatine (8g or one sachet) is about the same as four gelatine leaves. The two types are interchangable but leaf gelatine gives a much clearer mixture than dried gelatine.

GINGER also known as green or root ginger; the thick root of a tropical plant.

glacé fresh ginger root preserved in sugar syrup. Crystallised ginger can be substituted if rinsed with warm water and dried before using.

ground also known as powdered ginger; cannot be substituted for fresh ginger.

GLACE FRUIT fruit such as cherries, peaches, pineapple and orange cooked in heavy sugar syrup then dried.

GLUCOSE SYRUP also known as liquid glucose, made from wheat or corn starch.

GOLDEN SYRUP a by-product of refined sugarcane; pure maple syrup or honey can be substituted.

HAZELNUTS, GROUND also known as hazelnut meal; is made by grounding the hazelnuts to a coarse flour texture for use in baking or as a thickening agent.

HORSERADISH a vegetable with edible green leaves but mainly grown for its long, pungent white root. Horseradish cream is a commercially prepared creamy paste consisting of grated horseradish, vinegar, oil and sugar.

ICING SUGAR see sugar.

LIQUEURS & SPIRITS

orange-flavoured we use Grand Marnier.

coconut-flavoured we use Malibu.

MAPLE SYRUP a thin syrup distilled from the sap of the maple tree. Maple-flavoured syrup or pancake syrup is not an adequate substitute for the real thing.

MIXED PEEL candied citrus peel.

MIXED SPICE a blend of ground spices usually consisting of cinnamon, allspice and nutmeg.

MUSCAT also known as muscatel; refers to both the grape variety and the sweet dessert wine made from it. The grape is superb eaten fresh; when dried, its distinctively musty flavour goes well with cheese, chocolate, pork and game. In winemaking, the grape is used for Italian Asti Spumante, a range of Australian fortifieds, Metaxa from Greece and so on.

MUSTARD

english an extremely hot powdered mustard. A mild variety is also available.

PAPAYA also known as pawpaw; large, pear-shaped red-orange tropical fruit.

PARSLEY, FLAT-LEAF also known as continental or italian parsley.

PASTRY

puff pastry packaged ready-rolled sheets of frozen puff pastry, available from supermarkets.

shortcrust pastry packaged ready-rolled sheets of frozen shortcrust pastry, available from supermarkets.

PORK

fillet skinless, boneless eye-fillet cut from the loin.

PRESERVED LEMON RIND lemons are quartered and preserved in salt and lemon juice or water. To use, remove and discard pulp, squeeze juice from rind, rinse rind well; slice thinly. Sold in jars or singly by delicatessens; once opened, store under refrigeration.

PUMPERNICKEL a coarse, dark coloured sweet-sour bread made primarily of rye flour. Molasses is often added to give strong flavour and colour.

RAISINS dried sweet grapes.

READY-MADE WHITE ICING also known as soft icing, ready-to-roll and prepared fondant.

RUM we use a dark underproof rum (not overproof) for a more subtle flavour in cooking. White rum is almost colourless, sweet and used mostly in mixed drinks.

SAUCES

char siu also called Chinese barbecue sauce; a paste-like ingredient dark-red-brown in colour with a sharp sweet and spicy flavour. Made with fermented soybeans, honey and various spices; can be diluted and used as a marinade or brushed onto grilling meat.

soy made from fermented soya beans. Several variations are available in most supermarkets and Asian food stores.

light soy fairly thin in consistency and, while paler than the others, the saltiest tasting; used in dishes in which the natural colour of the ingredients is to be maintained. Not to be confused with salt-reduced or low-sodium soy sauces.

Tabasco brand name of an extremely fiery sauce made from vinegar, thai red chillies and salt.

worcestershire a dark coloured sauce made from garlic, soy sauce, tamarind, onions, molasses, lime, anchovies, vinegar and seasonings.

SHERRY fortified wine consumed as an aperitif or used in cooking. Sherries differ in colour and flavour;

sold as fino (light, dry), amontillado (medium sweet, dark) and oloroso (full-bodied, very dark).

STAR ANISE a dried star-shaped fruit of a tree native to China. The pods have an astringent aniseed or licorice flavour. Available whole and ground.

SUGAR

caster also known as superfine or finely granulated table sugar.

icing also known as confectioners' sugar or powdered sugar; granulated sugar crushed together with a small amount of added cornflour.

light brown also known simply as brown, a soft, finely granulated sugar retaining molasses for its characteristic colour and flavour.

pure icing also known as confectioners' sugar or powdered sugar, but has no added cornflour.

white a coarse, granulated table sugar, also known as crystal sugar.

SULTANAS dried grapes, also known as golden raisins.

TREACLE thick, dark syrup not unlike molasses; a by-product of sugar refining.

TURKISH DELIGHT extremely popular Middle Eastern sweet. Its Turkish name is rahat lokum – meaning 'rest for the throat'. A mixture of syrup and cornflour is boiled with either honey or fruit juice. Most often flavoured with rosewater or peppermint. Available from supermarkets.

VANILLA

bean dried long, thin pod from a tropical golden orchid; the tiny black seeds impart a luscious vanilla flavour in baking and desserts. A whole bean can be placed in a

sugar container to make the vanilla sugar often called for in recipes.

extract made by pulping chopped vanilla beans with a mixture of alcohol and water. This gives a very strong solution, so only a couple of drops are needed.

VIETNAMESE MINT not a mint at all, but a pungent and peppery narrow-leafed member of the buckwheat family; also known as cambodian mint and laksa leaf.

VINEGAR

red wine made from red wine.

WHEATEN CORNFLOUR see cornflour.

WITLOF also known as endive; cigar-shaped, tightly packed heads with pale, yellow-green tips. Has a delicately bitter flavour. May be cooked or eaten raw.

WOMBOK also known as peking or chinese cabbage or petsai. Elongated in shape with pale green, crinkly leaves, this is the most common cabbage in South-East Asian cooking.

WONTON WRAPPERS and gow gee or spring roll pastry sheets, made of flour, egg and water, are found in the refrigerated or freezer section of Asian food shops and many supermarkets. These come in different thicknesses and shapes. Thin wrappers work best in soups, while the thicker ones are best for frying; and the choice of round or square, small or large is dependent on the recipe.

ZUCCHINI also known as courgette; small, pale- or dark-green, yellow or white vegetable belonging to the squash family. If harvested young, its edible flowers can be baked or fried.

CONVERSION CHART

MEASURES

One Australian metric measuring cup holds approximately 250ml, one Australian metric tablespoon holds 20ml, one Australian metric teaspoon holds 5ml.

The difference between one country's measuring cups and another's is within a 2- or 3-teaspoon variance, and will not affect your cooking results. North America, New Zealand and the United Kingdom use a 15ml tablespoon. All cup and spoon measurements are level. The most accurate way of measuring dry ingredients is to weigh them. When measuring liquids, use a clear glass or plastic jug with metric markings.

We use large eggs with an average weight of 60g.

DRY MEASURES

METRIC	IMPERIAL
15g	½oz
30g	1oz
60g	2oz
90g	3oz
125g	4oz (¼lb)
155g	5oz
185g	6oz
220g	7oz
250g	8oz (½lb)
280g	9oz
315g	10oz
345g	11oz
375g	12oz (¾lb)
410g	13oz
440g	14oz
470g	15oz
500g	16oz (1lb)
750g	24oz (1½lb)
1kg	32oz (2lb)

LIQUID MEASURES

METRIC	IMPERIAL
30ml	1 fluid oz
60ml	2 fluid oz
100ml	3 fluid oz
125ml	4 fluid oz
150ml	5 fluid oz
190ml	6 fluid oz
250ml	8 fluid oz
300ml	10 fluid oz
500ml	16 fluid oz
600ml	20 fluid oz
1000ml (1 litre)	1¾ pints

LENGTH MEASURES

METRIC	IMPERIAL
3mm	⅛in
6mm	¼in
1cm	½in
2cm	¾in
2.5cm	1in
5cm	2in
6cm	2½in
8cm	3in
10cm	4in
13cm	5in
15cm	6in
18cm	7in
20cm	8in
23cm	9in
25cm	10in
28cm	11in
30cm	12in (1ft)

OVEN TEMPERATURES

These oven temperatures are only a guide for conventional ovens. For fan-forced ovens, check the manufacturer's manual.

	°C (CELSIUS)	°F (FAHRENHEIT)
Very slow	120	250
Slow	150	275-300
Moderately slow	160	325
Moderate	180	350-375
Moderately hot	200	400
Hot	220	425-450
Very hot	240	475

The imperial measurements used in these recipes are approximate only. Measurements for cake pans are approximate only. Using same-shaped cake pans of a similar size should not affect the outcome of your baking. We measure the inside top of the cake pan to determine sizes.

INDEX

First Published in 2011 by ACP Magazines Ltd,

a division of Nine Entertainment Co.

54 Park St, Sydney

GPO Box 4088, Sydney, NSW 2001.

phone (02) 9282 8618; fax (02) 9126 3702

acpbooks@acpmagazines.com.au; www.acpbooks.com.au

ACP BOOKS

General Manager · Christine Whiston

Editor-in-Chief · Susan Tomnay

Creative Director · Hieu Chi Nguyen

Food Director · Pamela Clark

Published and Distributed in the United Kingdom by Octopus Publishing Group

Endeavour House

189 Shaftesbury Avenue

London WC2H 8JY

United Kingdom

phone (+44)(0)207 632 5400; fax (+44)(0)207 632 5405

info@octopus-publishing.co.uk;

www.octopusbooks.co.uk

Printed by Toppan Printing Co., China

International foreign language rights, Brian Cearnes, ACP Books bcearnes@acpmagazines.com.au

A catalogue record for this book is available from the British Library.

ISBN 978-1-74245-088-9